Journey

to

Success

Written by Joseph L. Neely
Cover Photo © Corel Stock Photo Library / Corel Corporation
Cover Design by Dmitry Feygin

Published by Great Quotations Publishing Co., Glendale Heights, IL

Library of Congress Catalog Card Number: 96-078970

ISBN 1-56245-285-1

Printed in Hong Kong

For Dean Warner,
who hit the bumps hard
but somehow
got back on the road,
and for everyone
trying to do the same thing.

Thomas S. Monaghan

Thomas S. Monaghan's father died on Christmas Eve when Monaghan was just four years old. Although his mother was alive and visited her sons often, financial uncertainty forced her to place Monaghan and his brother in St. Joseph's Home for Boys, an orphanage in Jackson, Michigan. While at the orphanage, Monaghan had two childhood dreams; playing shortstop for the Detroit Tigers and becoming a priest. Monaghan studied for the priesthood as a teenager, but was asked to leave the seminary after less than one year. After some early successes in the pizza business, Monaghan's Domino's Pizza barely avoided bankruptcy in the early 1970's, and Monaghan temporarily lost control of the company to creditors.

Overcoming Obstacles

Thomas S. Monaghan

By 1993 Domino's had consolidated its position as one of the nation's largest pizza chains, with sales of $2.2 billion. Although he never became the team's shortstop, Tom Monaghan eventually bought the Detroit Tigers. The team won the World Series in 1984, Monaghan's first year as owner. He has since sold the team. Monaghan remains the President of Domino's Pizza.

On The Journey To Success

Robert James Waller's novel, <u>The Bridges of Madison County</u>, was rejected by several publishers before being accepted by Warner Books.

*T*he novel, Waller's first, was to become the largest selling hardcover novel in American publishing history. Waller's second novel, _Slow Waltz in Cedar Bend_, has also become a bestseller. In addition, Robert James Waller recently released a recording of original songs.

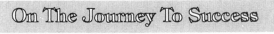

Gloria Steinem

Gloria Steinem was just a young girl when her father divorced his wife and left home. Steinem spent her teenage years caring for her mentally ill mother in a house they shared with rats and poverty. As a co-founder of Ms. magazine in 1972, Steinem fought a constant battle to convince advertisers to spend their money in a publication considered too radical by some. In 1986, Steinem underwent surgery to remove a malignant tumor in her breast.

Overcoming Obstacles

Gloria Steinem

Gloria Steinem became one of America's most famous feminists and political activists. She has written several bestselling books in recent years, most recently <u>Revolution From Within: A Book of Self-Esteem</u>.

On The Journey To Success

Robert **Frost** is perhaps America's best known and most loved poet. Although he achieved some success as a young man with his poetry, by 1921 Frost found himself approaching fifty and earning almost nothing from his writing. In three years he had sold only one new poem—and that for the grand total of $30 dollars.

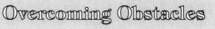

*O*n one extraordinarily productive June night in 1922, Frost stayed up until dawn writing the title poem for his Pulitzer Prize winning volume of poetry, "New Hampshire." The poet took a short break and then resumed his writing. The result was his most famous poem, "Stopping by Woods on a Snowy Evening." Frost went on to achieve enormous success, including another Pulitzer Prize and accepting an invitation to read his poetry at the inauguration of President John F. Kennedy.

Rush Limbaugh

Rush **Limbaugh** flunked a speech class in high school. In 1971 he was fired from a radio station in Pittsburgh and advised to consider switching to sales, in light of the fact he didn't appear to have the talent necessary for an on-air position. He was later fired by two different major radio stations in Kansas City.

Overcoming Obstacles

Rush Limbaugh

*L*imbaugh's syndicated show has become the most listened to show in the history of American radio, with an estimated 20 million listeners tuning in daily. In recent years, Limbaugh has written two bestselling books, while his syndicated TV show has also become enormously popular and successful.

On The Journey To Success

W hat's left to be said about **Abraham Lincoln**? He was desperately poor, often hungry, accustomed to back-breaking work, and self-educated. Lincoln lost the first election in which he was a candidate. Several business ventures he was involved in went bankrupt, leaving Lincoln struggling under a crushing burden of debt. He tried and failed to secure the Whig Party's nomination for Congress several times before being nominated in 1846. Lincoln failed in two attempts to win election to the U. S. Senate; his second attempt in 1858 featured the famous debates with Stephen A. Douglas.

*M*any, *if not most, historians rate Lincoln as our greatest President. His vision is credited with preserving the Union in the aftermath of the Civil War. The simplicity and eloquence of Lincoln's Gettysburg Address ensure that the speech will endure forever.*

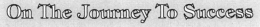

Wally Amos

Wally Amos had it all, and then he lost it all. In 1975 he opened the country's first gourmet cookie store, and in just a few years his company's sales were approaching $100 million. While Wally Amos' face and Panama hat were known to millions of Americans, a lack of professional management resulted in his losing control of the company he founded. Financial difficulties also resulted in foreclosure proceedings being instituted against his home. After protracted litigation, Wally Amos found himself unable to use his own name or likeness in connection with any new business venture.

Overcoming Obstacles

Wally Amos

*W*ally Amos' book, <u>*The Man With No Name: Turning Lemons Into Lemonade*</u>, *details his triumph over adversity. Although still facing a substantial amount of debt, Wally Amos says "It's only debt." Famous Amos contends that Americans need to change their mindset and realize that hard times are meant to be overcome, not to destroy us. In good times and bad Wally Amos never quit giving of himself to others, a fact which he credits with keeping himself focused and in touch with what truly matters in life. He concluded a recent interview by saying, "There's always someone who's got it worse than you do. Get off your duff, get on with it, take charge of your life."*

On The Journey To Success

Alaska's Iditarod Trail Sled Dog Race covers 1,158 grueling miles, from Anchorage to Nome. Most men and women wouldn't think of putting themselves through what it takes to run the Iditarod. **Martin Buser** endured the numbing cold, along with the mental and physical exhaustion, of the Iditarod eight times without tasting victory.

*I*n his ninth attempt, Martin Buser not only won the Iditarod but also smashed the northern course record by almost seven hours. Buser set another record while winning the Iditarod again in 1994.

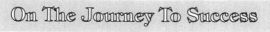

W. Michael Blumenthal

As a young man, **W. Michael Blumenthal's** family's business was seized by the Nazis. The family fled Germany for Shanghai in 1939, and remained there as refugees for the duration of World War II. For two years while in Shanghai, the family was held in a Japanese internment camp. Blumenthal immigrated to the United States in 1947 when he was twentyone years old, arriving with less than $60 in his pocket.

Overcoming Obstacles

W. Michael Blumenthal

*W.**Michael Blumenthal earned three graduate degrees after arriving in the United States, including a PhD in economics from Princeton University. His distinguished career in business has included serving as President of the Bendix Corporation, and as President and C.E.O. of Unisys. Blumenthal served as Treasury Secretary under President Jimmy Carter from 1977–79.*

On The Journey To Success

Racial discrimination kept black Americans out of major league baseball until Brooklyn Dodger President Branch Rickey signed **Jackie Robinson** to a minor league contract in 1945. In 1947 Robinson became the first black American to play in the majors. In the early years of his career, Robinson was often thrown at by pitchers, spiked by baserunners, and subjected to racial taunts by fans and players alike. Robinson received many death threats, and also received threats that his infant son would be kidnapped. To keep a promise he had made to Rickey, Robinson did not respond to racial provocations during his first season.

Jackie Robinson

*J*ackie Robinson was voted National League Rookie of the Year in 1947. Among the many honors he earned were being named to six National League All-Star Teams, and being named the league's Most Valuable Player in 1949. Robinson was elected to the Baseball Hall of Fame in 1962, his first year of eligibility.

On The Journey To Success

Frederick Douglass

Frederick Douglass was born a slave. Like most slave children, he was taken from his mother in order to prevent a parent-child bond from forming. When he was a young boy, his master's wife was chastized for teaching him to recognize a few letters of the alphabet, and thereafter Frederick Douglass received no formal training in reading or writing. Sold as chattel from one owner to another, he was often beaten. Frederick Douglass was imprisoned for his role in a plan by slaves to escape to freedom.

Overcoming Obstacles

Frederick Douglass

Frederick Douglass secretly learned to read and write by talking with white children and observing the carpenters in a shipyard where he worked as a slave. In 1838 he escaped to the North, and within a few years was lecturing on the evils of slavery. In 1845 Douglass' autobiography was published, and in 1847 the man who was forbidden to read or write founded an abolitionist newspaper. Frederick Douglass recruited black soldiers for the Union Army during the Civil War, and continued to fight inequality throughout his life. Frederick Douglass, born into slavery, went on to serve as Recorder of Deeds for the District of Columbia, and as U. S. Minister to Haiti.

On The Journey To Success

Michael Jordan

Michael **Jordan** was cut twice from the varsity basketball team at Laney High School in Wilmington, North Carolina.

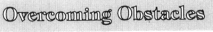

In 1982, Michael Jordan made the winning shot as the Univeristy of North Carolina won the NCAA Basketball Tournament. Michael Jordan capped his amateur basketball career by leading the American team to a gold medal in the 1984 Summer Olympic Games. He went on to become the greatest player in the history of professional basketball. Air Jordan won the National Basketball Association's Most Valuable Player Award three times, and was the Most Valuable Player in the National Basketball (NBA) Association finals while leading the Bulls to the NBA Championship in 1991, 1992, and 1993.

Tina Turner

Tina **Turner** achieved great musical success while singing with Ike Turner, including a Grammy Award in 1976 for their rendition of "Proud Mary." To escape an abusive relationship with her husband, however, in 1976 Tina Turner fled into the night with only 36¢ and a gasoline credit card in her pocket. While attempting to establish a solo career, Turner supported herself by cleaning houses and with food stamps. Her early solo recordings were not commercially successful, and Tina Turner remained deeply in debt as a result of performances that were cancelled when she left her husband.

Overcoming Obstacles

Tina Turner

*T*ina Turner won a fistful of awards for her 1984 album "Private Dancer," including two Grammy Awards and two American Music Awards. In 1993 Touchstone Pictures released the story of Tina Turner's life, "What's Love Got to Do With it." Tina Turner is a member of the Rock 'n Roll Hall of Fame.

On The Journey To Success

W hen he was a student in 5th grade, **Les Brown** was mistakenly labelled as being "educably mentally retarded." Overcoming this stigma, he achieved his dream of becoming successful in radio only to be fired when the station's management decided he was too controversial. Determined to establish a career as a motivational speaker, Les Brown slept on the floor of his Detroit office because he couldn't afford an apartment.

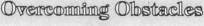

*L*es Brown has become one of the most successful motivational speakers in America. In 1989 he was awarded the National Speakers Association's highest award, and in 1992 he was named one of America's top speakers by Toastmasters International. Brown is also a bestselling author and the host of a syndicated television show.

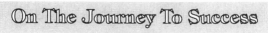

Philip Zazove

Philip Zazove was born practically deaf. In spite of the fact that he excelled as an undergraduate at Northwestern University, Zazove was rejected by a host of medical schools—the same schools that accepted his classmates with lower grades and test scores. Unable to find a medical school willing to take a chance on a practically deaf student, and unwilling to give up his life-long dream of becoming a doctor, Philip Zazove spent a year at Northwestern's graduate school of biology in a last attempt to demonstrate his worthiness to medical schools.

Overcoming Obstacles

Philip Zazove

*P*hilip Zazove was ultimately accepted to Rutger University's medical school, and later transferred to Washington University. His book, <u>When the Phone Rings, My Bed Shakes</u>, details the many obstacles he has overcome enroute to becoming a successful family practitioner in Ann Arbor, Michigan.

On The Journey To Success

W hen **John H. Johnson** sought to publish his first magazine, The Negro Digest, he was turned down by lenders who didn't believe a publication aimed at black Americans could be profitable. Johnson was forced to pledge his mother's furniture as collateral for a $500 loan, which he used to solicit prepaid subscriptions to The Negro Digest.

*T*he Negro Digest was the beginning of John H. Johnson's success in the publishing business. Johnson Publishing Company, Inc., publishes several magazines, including Ebony and Jet. Johnson Publishing Company subsidiaries are involved in broadcasting, TV production, cosmetics, and hair care products. Sales for 1993 exceeded $290 million.

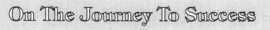

Phil Knight

When **Phil Knight** started his new business, he sold running shoes from the trunk of his car. Strapped for cash, the company was once forced to forego entering into a contract with tennis star Jimmy Connors when Connors' agent demanded the paltry sum of $1500. Not only was the company unable to borrow new money, but its existing loan was called by a bank which also threatened to cause Knight's company to be prosecuted for bouncing checks.

Overcoming Obstacles

Phil Knight

The company Phil Knight started, Nike, recently reported sales in excess of $3.7 billion. The days when Nike couldn't afford Jimmy Connor's meager asking price are long gone: Nike now has multi-million dollar endorsement deals with athletes such as Michael Jordan, Bo Jackson, Deion Sanders, Charles Barkley, and Jim Courier. Nike employs approximately 6,500 people, and in 1993 the Sporting News named Phil Knight the most powerful person in sports.

On The Journey To Success

James Carville didn't enter the field of political consulting until he was in his mid-thirties. In 1982 his candidate lost in the first statewide campaign Carville managed. Carville followed this effort up by managing the losing 1984 campaign of a candidate for the U. S. Senate from Texas.

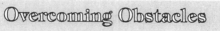

*I*n 1992 Carville masterminded the strategy that helped Bill Clinton unseat an incumbent President of the United States. Carville is perhaps best known for the focus he provided to Clinton's campaign: "It's the economy, stupid."

Vanessa Williams

On Sept. 14, 1983, **Vanessa Williams** was crowned Miss America; the first African-American woman to be so honored. The next year, however, she relinquished her crown when it was announced that Penthouse magazine would publish revealing photos taken while Williams had worked as a photographer's assistant. In discussing her resignation, Williams told an interviewer from People magazine that ". . . this would have to be the worst thing that has happened in my life. . . I've hit rock bottom."

Overcoming Obstacles

Vanessa Williams

Refusing to allow public embarrassment to set the tone for her life, Vanessa Williams honed the acting and singing skills which had helped her to win the Miss America crown in the first place. Four years after relinquishing her crown, Williams' first album went gold in sales. In 1991 Williams achieved her first number one hit, "Save the Best for Last." In 1994 Vanessa Williams realized a long-cherished dream by performing on Broadway in the role of Aurora in "Kiss of the Spider Woman." Happily married and the mother of three children, Vanessa Williams' life since relinquishing her crown is living proof the old adage that living well is the best revenge.

On The Journey To Success

Tim Allen

In 1979, **Tim Allen** was arrested and charged with distribution of cocaine. He pleaded guilty at his arraignment, and started performing at local comedy clubs while waiting to be sentenced. Tim Allen was eventually sentenced to eight years in prison, and credits his ability to make people laugh with helping him to get along with other inmates in prison. He was released, with time off for good behavior, after twenty-eight months.

Overcoming Obstacles

Tim Allen

After paying his debt to society, Tim Allen put the mistakes he made as a young man behind him. Allen has gone on to achieve spectacular success as a comedian and actor, most notably in the starring role on ABC's top-rated series "Home Improvement."

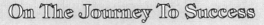

Dick Vitale

Dick **Vitale** was an extremely success-ful basketball coach at the high school and college levels. At the professional level, however, Vitale did not meet with much success. During the 1978–79 season, Vitale's Detroit Pistons struggled to a 30–52 record. Vitale was fired early in the 1979–80 season after the Pistons got off to a disastrous start. Dick Vitale was devastat-ed by his firing, certain that he would never work in basketball again.

Overcoming Obstacles

Dick Vitale

Dick Vitale seems to be everywhere these days. In addition to providing color commentary for college basketball on radio and TV, Vitale is an author and publishes pre-season basketball magazines. He is also much in demand as a motivational speaker.

Roy **Orbison** had achieved world-wide acclaim for his music in the early 1960's, including hit songs like "Pretty Woman," "Crying," "Only the Lonely," and "Blue Bayou." By the middle of that decade, however, his popularity had receded in the face of the British invasion. Devastating personal tragedies also struck Orbison during that period. In 1966 his first wife was struck by a truck and killed as she and Orbison rode their motorcycles together. In 1968, two of Orbison's three children died in a fire which also destroyed his home.

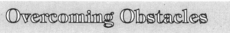

*W*ith the help of his second wife, Barbara, Orbison rebuilt his personal and professional life. Orbison recorded a string of successful albums in the 1970's and 1980's, and won a Grammy Award in 1981 for a duet he recorded with Emmylou Harris. At the time of his death in 1988, Orbison was in great demand as a solo performer. He was also a member of The Travelling Wilburys, a band which included Bob Dylan, George Harrison, Tom Petty, and Jeff Lynne.

Mary Kay Ash

Frustrated by jobs where she felt she was unfairly denied promotions and her ideas were not listened to because of her sex, **Mary Kay Ash** made plans to start a new business with her husband. A month before the new business was to open, Mary Kay Ash's husband collapsed and died from a heart attack. Her financial advisors strongly discouraged her from going into business alone.

Overcoming Obstacles

Mary Kay Ash

In 1963, Mary Kay Ash began a company called Beauty By Mary Kay, the forerunner of Mary Kay Cosmetics. In her early years as a business owner, Mary Kay Ash ran the company from her home. Her children helped her to package orders, working at the family's kitchen table. Mary Kay Cosmetic's annual sales now exceed $600 million, and the company has a sales force of 300,000 women (and a few men!). Mary Kay Ash is the Chairman Emeritus of Mary Kay Cosmetics.

On The Journey To Success

*S*ally **Jessy Raphael** was fired from eighteen different jobs in broadcasting. Strapped for cash, she and her family were once forced to live in their car and supplement their income with food stamps.

*N*ever *losing sight of her dreams, and working incredibly long days, Sally Jessy Raphael hasn't been fired for a long time. Her nationally-syndicated TV show has been on the air for more than ten years. The show has won two Emmy's, including one for Best Talk-Show Host. Almost as proof that success, no matter how long in coming, does not protect one from the bumps in life's road, Sally Jessy Raphael was forced to endure the severe injury of one child in an auto accident and the death of her firstborn child in 1992. Perhaps by calling on the same determination that saw her reach the top of her chosen profession, Sally Jessy Raphael is in the process of moving on with her life.*

Cecil Fielder

Cecil Fielder's baseball career did not at first soar like the balls he smashes over the fence for the Detroit Tigers. When his son was born in 1984, Fielder was toiling in the minor leagues for a small salary and $12 per day in meal money. Fielder's wife, Stacey, worked three jobs to help keep the family fed. By 1985, Fielder had made up his mind to quit baseball so that he could support his family. Even when Cecil Fielder decided to give baseball another chance, he couldn't find a regular spot in the Toronto Blue Jay's lineup.

Overcoming Obstacles

Cecil Fielder

*C*ecil Fielder played the 1989 season in Japan, attracting the Detroit Tiger's attention by hitting thirty-eight home runs that year. Fielder hit 51 home runs for the Tigers in 1990, and led the majors again in 1991 with 44 homers. In 1993 Fielder signed a 5-year deal with Detroit, which is believed to pay him about $7 million a year; a far cry from the days his wife worked three jobs to keep food on the Fielder's table.

On The Journey To Success

T he path to failure stretched invitingly before **Ben Carson**. Abandoned by his father when he was eight years old, Carson did poorly in school. Even though he became a good student when his mother forced him to read and write reports on two books per week, Carson was still ruled by an uncontrollable temper. At the age of fourteen, Carson tried to stab a friend with whom he had argued over a transistor radio.

*F*ortunately for the world, Ben Carson's friend wore a large belt buckle, on which the knife struck and broke. That incident made Carson realize his need for self-control, and he turned to his faith for help. Carson earned a scholarship to Yale University and went on to graduate from the University of Michigan Medical School. In 1984 Ben Carson became the chief of pediatric neurosurgery at Johns Hopkins Hospital in Baltimore, one of the country's most prestigious hospitals.

Charles W. Colson

Charles W. Colson went from the big time to just plain doing time. As special assistant to President Richard Nixon, Colson had an insider's view of how power is wielded at the highest level. Like several of his colleagues in the Nixon White House, Colson became entangled in the Watergate scandal. Charles Colson eventually served seven months in prison for obstruction of justice.

Overcoming Obstacles

Charles W. Colson

*C*harles Colson experienced a dramatic conversion to Christianity while in prison. Using the proceeds from his 1976 autobiography, Colson established the Prison Fellowship Ministries in order to bring the Gospel's message of hope to prisoners and their families. In 1993, Colson was awarded the prestigious Templeton Prize for Progress in Religion. Previous winners of the Templeton Prize have included Reverend Billy Graham and Mother Teresa.

On The Journey To Success

Samantha Abeel hated seventh grade. Unable to comprehend even the simplest mathematical concepts - telling time, counting coins, arranging the numbers in her street address - Samantha felt like a failure. Many nights, Samantha cried and suffered through panic attacks; reactions to the difficulties she was experiencing at school.

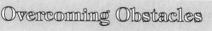

*W*orking with a very special teacher, Roberta Williams, Samantha worked on what would eventually become her book, <u>Reach for the Moon.</u> The book won the 1994 Margo Marek Award, given annually to the best book written on the subject of learning disabilities.

Samantha is a learning disabled special education student. "Special education changed my life," Samatha says in <u>Reach for the Moon.</u> She begins her book by writing: "A tree that stands in the moonlight reflects the light, yet also casts a shadow. People are the same. They have gifts that let them shine, yet they also have disabilities. . .This is my reflection of the light. Welcome to my book."

Julie Krone

Julie Krone is the first woman jockey to win a Triple Crown race in 1993 when she brought Colonial Affair home first in the Belmont Stakes. Later that year she became only the third jockey to win five races in one day at Saratoga Race Course in New York. On August 30, 1993, Julie Krone was involved in a racing accident that left her terribly injured. Her ankle was broken in eleven places, a gash in her elbow exposed the bone, and a kick in the chest from a trailing horse would likely have been fatal if not for the protective vest Krone wore. In addition to the constant physical pain which accompanied her injuries, Julie Krone's recovery forced her to overcome nightmares, depression, and doubt concerning her future in racing.

Overcoming Obstacles

Julie Krone

On May 26, 1994, Julie Krone resumed her winning ways by piloting a filly named Consider the Lily to victory at Belmont Park.

On The Journey To Success

Former First Lady **Betty Ford** was bitterly disappointed when her husband lost the 1976 presidential election to Jimmy Carter. Mrs. Ford also experienced severe health problems in the form of a pinched nerve in her neck and breast cancer. Partly as a reaction to these problems, Betty Ford began to abuse alcohol and prescription medications.

Mrs. Ford's family confronted her about her addictions to alcohol and prescription drugs in 1978. One by one they described the many ways in which she had let them down while under the influences of addictive substances. Had Mrs. Ford refused to seek help in battling her addictions, the family was prepared to cut off all further contact with her.

*M*rs. *Ford checked into a rehabilitation program shortly after being confronted by her family. Although battling addictions requires constant vigilance, she has remained clean and sober since that time. Sensing the critical need for addiction treatment facilities, Mrs. Ford headed a $7.6 million drive to raise funds for The Betty Ford Center, a chemical dependency center in Rancho Mirage, California.*

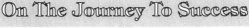

Author Joseph L. Neely,
is a successful small businessman
and former radio talk show host.
He lives in Ann Arbor, Michigan and
recently returned to school
to pursue his dream of becoming an
English teacher.